Rockpeople

THE CHESTER CREEK
INUKSUIT ANTHOLOGY

Words, Inuksuit, & Photos by
Joel Carter

Canukshuk Artworks
2001 East Fouth Street
Duluth, Minnesota 55812
218-728-5737

Rockpeople: the Chester Creek inuksuit anthology

Text, Inksuit, and Photographs by Joel Carter
Cover and interior design by Tony Dierckins

First Edition, 2004

04 05 06 07 08 • 5 4 3 2 1

ISBN: 0-9745847-0-3

Printed in Singapore by TWP America

Publishing consultation provided by:

www.x-communication.org

For the memory and lives of my grandparents
Waclaw Reicher and Janina Reicher, my cousin Tadeuz Rothenthal,
and my other relatives who perished in the horror of the
Holocaust in Poland during World War II.

↬

I would like to acknowledge my tribe of family and friends who have
supported my journey with love and companionship. I have received
no greater gift then that of my family and friends as well as the big
medicine teachers who have appeared in my life.

To my inner circle of sacred sojourners
for continuing to love and provide a container
for my life experience and expression.

Specifically, I wish to express my heart felt gratitude to Chris Herman
for the journey years together and who through her life first manifest
for me an appreciation that art is everywhere, that the rocks do
truly speak, and encouraged me find its expression within.

To Larry Cooley who was my first "big medicine" teacher by way
of the numinous quality of his soul, intellect and compassion,
and who awoke in me the quest for meaning and understanding
of the human spiritual experience.

My special thanks to June Kallestad, Greg Bernhardt, Dena Cyr,
and Tony Dierckins for their input, editing, and smiles.

To Joan Christensen who inspired the project, made it creatively
possible, and taught me the life lesson of non-attachment.

And to the Ancestors—the Grandmother and Grandfather Spirits
and the Silent Ones—much gratitude for all what is in my life.

Introduction

A number of years ago on the beaches of Sanibel Island, my former wife Chris revealed to me that the rocks and stones "spoke" to her. I didn't know what to do, except stare down at the beach rocks at my feet and say "hello." Nothing happened. "Hello!" I repeated. Silence again....

A few years later in a sweat lodge in the area around Taos, New Mexico, I asked the water pourer, "How do men move from head to heart?" Guy Red Owl replied, "You learn from the women, and listen to the rocks." And in the coming months and years things began to happen that shifted my center to my heart.

Marion Woodman, well-known author and Jungian, has said that one has two choices in undertaking such a journey. Either you can muster up as much dignity as possible and walk into the encounter by conscious choice and courage—or you will be dragged there kicking and screaming like a trussed pig. I would like to think I was a well-composed initiate, but my resistive clutching and clawing at the earth speaks more to the former experience.

I have since had the privilege of spending time with the female tribe in a number of circumstances, being taught and guided by their experiences, their grief, and losses. It has been one of the most enriching and healing experiences of my soul, and I am indebted to my many female mentors and teachers who have opened their hearts to me with much wisdom, love, and compassion.

I also began building rock cairns on the north shore of Lake Superior not far from my home in Duluth, Minnesota, hoping the rocks might begin "speaking." The cairns transformed into what I understood to be inuksuit, Inuit rock structures meaning "Man of Stone that points the way."

According to the work of Norman Hallendy, "things that we call inuksuit were built all over the world in ancient times. They just had different names because they were built by people who spoke other languages. These stone figures, like the ones built by the Inuit, were helpers to the early hunters and travelers. Plural for Inuk, Inuit is the Inuktitut word for 'human beings.' For thousands of years, Arctic North America has been the home of the Inuit. Except for a very few places in the world, these ancient helpers are gone and now forgotten. If inuksuit could speak, they would tell us stories of the time when humans were a part of nature and not yet so separated from it as we have come to be.

"An inuksuk is a stone structure that can communicate knowledge essential for survival to an Arctic traveler. Inuksuit [plural] are found throughout the Arctic area of Alaska, Canada, and Greenland. Inuksuit have been used by the Inuit to act in place of human messengers. For those who understand their forms, inuksuit in the Arctic are very important helpers, they show direction, tell about a good hunting or fishing area, show where food is stored, indicate a good resting place or act as a message center.

"Every inuksuk is unique because it is built from the stones at hand. Inuksuit can be small or large; a single rock put in place; several rocks balanced on top of each other; boulders placed in a pile; or flat stones stacked. One of these stone structures is known as an inuksuk, two are called inuksuuk, and three or more are referred to as inuksuit.

"An inuksuk is a strong connection to the land; it is built on the land, it is made of the land and it tells about the land. Inuit are taught to be respectful of inuksuit. There is a traditional law, which persists today, that forbids damaging or destroying inuksuit in any way. New inuksuit can be built to mark the presence of modern-day Inuit, but the old ones should never be touched. Traditionally, it is said that if one destroys an inuksuk, his or her life will be cut shorter.

"Over time, the style of building inuksuit has changed. In the past, most inuksuit were built by stacking rock in a particular way, but usually not in the shape of a human. However, many modern inuksuit are built to look like human figures made of stone (with a head, body, arms, and legs). In Inuktitut, these are called inunnguaq. Some Inuit believe that this type of stone figure was first built about one hundred years ago, after the arrival of qallunaat (non-Inuit) whalers. Others say that this human look-alike originated long before this century."

I began to realize inuksuit are powerful art forms as well as compelling teachers about balance, control, and how the integrity of the structure is dependent on the "broken shards" which provide stability to the completed form. The inuksuit seem to me to be a compelling metaphor for life and the human soul's journey, and shape-shifted the universal experience of "the broken places" into something that has purpose and meaning.

In the Fall of 2000, I had a significant trip to Poland with my father, a Holocaust survivor. I had never been to Poland. It will perhaps be the most important journey I will ever take in this life. There were many incredible unfoldings on many levels. One of the most significant was when we entered the remanent of Treblinka—the extermination camp that murdered 800,000 Jews, a majority from the Warsaw Ghetto, including my grandmother and perhaps my grandfather, although he may have died in the Warsaw Ghetto Uprising.

Treblinka was a camp on the edge of nowhere in woods, not unlike those close to where I live. It was a sunny day with blue sky when my father and I visited the site after a long drive from Warsaw. The parking lot was deserted. There was a long walk towards the main camp site along where the loading dock once stood for the trains that unloaded their human cargo. Nothing remains of the tracks or railway ties except large stone ties that marked where the trains stopped. My father was ahead as I slowly strolled, thinking of the 800,000 human beings who were marched along this path decades ago.

As I turned into the central camp area where my father was already standing, I was stopped dead by what stood in front of me. In the bright sunlight and gentle breeze stood before me an expansive field overflowing with a multitude of upright stones and rocks. And as I gazed across the vastness, my eyes came to rest on a singular huge stone structure in the epicenter of the mass of rocks. It was, in essence, an inuksuk with a Menorah imprinted into the cap stones. And the rocks silently spoke in a way I could not have imagined or dreamed. In the midst of Treblinka, my Father by my side, I met my tribe for the first time—I had finally come home.

On two unmarked rocks, my Father and I performed a ritual dedication for his parents. Left behind were two burning candles, feathers, and two stones from the shores of Lake Superior.

This book is a continuance of my journey with rocks that first began with the words of Guy Red Owl who spoke to me of "listening to the rocks." The rocks remain a powerful presence in my life and continue to teach me about healing, compassion and non-attachment.

I hope this offering serves as an invitation to you to turn inward and be open to what the rocks may have to say to the deeper aspects of who you are.

— Joel Carter, 2003

The remnant of Treblinka, the extermination camp in Poland where the Nazis murdered 800,000 Jews, the majority from the Warsaw Ghetto. Victims included the author's grandmother and possibly his grandfather (his grandfather may have died in the Warsaw Ghetto Uprising). This photo was taken in autumn, 2000.

Sanctuary

Sacred Moments

I decided to stop
praying and instead consider
my whole life a prayer.

Now all my moments are sacred,
it's more time effective,
and my knees aren't so sore.

Pinnacle

Cannon-ball

There comes a time
when we have to fall into
the arms of the universe
whether we want to or not.

When that time comes we can
either jump or wait to be pushed.

Jumping seems to be the better option to me.

At least I can cannon-ball and make a bigger splash.

Apprentice

The Wind

Taking your chances with the wind
means you have to be prepared
for the parts of you that are
blown away,

as well as

those
that
are

uncovered.

Invocation

Spiritual Practice

After years of questioning and searching
I finally decided what my
spiritual practice is.

It's called life.

It's an all inclusive denomination.
The theology is dynamic, fluid,
and always changing.
The pulpit is everywhere.
The central doctrine is conscious love,
compassion, and awareness.
All contributions are mainstream
random acts of kindness.
And new members are always welcome.

Black Madonna

Emergence

Life isn't so much
about growing up
and out,
as it is about
emerging within.

Mourning

Deep Places

I don't think we are suppose to
"recover" from the deep places life takes us.

I think we are called to embrace
the darkness, the unknowing and
the joy of being alive.

All these call us into the mystery
of the soul's journey and its dream.

June

Bum Bites

She said, "I wonder if you
take life too seriously?"

I said, "What else is there
to be serious about?"

Then I turned her over
and bit her bum.

Morning Glory

My Moments

When I let go
of my fear
of tomorrow,
and held on
to being present
in all my moments,
I realized
I was happy,
and had
everything
I needed.

Extravagance

Mainstream

Why would I want to be mainstream?
God forbid that I should ever be mainstream!

Take Off

Flying

The best part
of letting go
is getting the
chance to see
if you can fly.

Sailing

May the compass of my life be mystery.

May my soul set sail with the thrill of adventure.

May I steer directly into the unknown

with my eyes wide open,

With my heart full —

Following my breath as it fills my sails.

Shaman

It

Some choose to run from it.

Some choose to ignore it.

Some people cover it up.

Some people pretend it doesn't exist.

I chose to dive into its center,

and in its silence

I changed.

Watchmen

The Soul's Gate

The heart and life's circumstances
eventually lead to the soul's gate.

The journey then is to unlatch the soul and open,
as opposed to jumping over the top
or sneaking underneath.

Suspended

The Questions

To find life's answers
I have to remember to raise my hand
to ask the questions.

Sometimes though —
my arm gets real tired.

Hanging On

Great View

The best part
about having
one's life up in
the air is that
it gives one a
great view of
everything else.

Magician

Balance Point

I've been stacking rocks
on the shore of Lake Superior
for the last number of months.
I've found that the rocks have
balance points that you can feel.

I've also found the higher the stack
gets the less control you have —
and you need to let the rocks find
the balance point themselves.

Proud Mother

Unfolding

It's often said
that the universe
is unfolding
as it should.

So I decided —
I am too.

Jedi

Instead

God forbid I should
forget to live my life,
and live someone else's
life instead.

Soul Mates

Sojourner

Getting older isn't
so much about being
a frequent flyer, as
it is about being a
seasoned sojourner.

You travel lighter,
learn life is full of accommodations,
your valuables are always with you,
and you come to love the unexpected
twists in the road.

On the Edge

The Details

I finally gave the details
to the Universe to work out.

It's been around
a lot longer
and probably
knows
what
it's
doing.

Safe Harbor

A Small Flame

I excavated
into the deep.

Sat there
with its
dark silence.

Danced that dance
of grief, pain,
and loss.

And after
sometime in the
vast cavity of my soul,
a small flame ignited.

And I saw you
were already
waiting there,
in the soft
tender chamber
of my heart.

Letting Go

Something Solid

Falling into the
abyss is not such
a bad thing.

After plummeting
through the darkness you
eventually hit something solid.

That's when the door
opens and you finally
know you're home.

Dancing

Dancing

She said she had
a gift for me
so I asked
what it was.

She said it was the gift
of woundedness,
and that it
was given
with love.

Then she smiled at me with
a twinkle in her eye
and began to dance.

And she danced,
and she danced
until she disappeared.
After sometime
I began to understand.

And then I began to dance too.

The Ancestors

More Room

Today I realized
all the anger and rage
were finally gone.
And there's so
much more room now
for everything else.

Indigenous

Instead

Instead of fearing my truth,
I decided I would start trusting it.

Silence

Sometimes it's important
not to say or think anything —
in order to let
the silence
speak the
truth.

The Grail Castle

The Call

At some point in life
we all have the opportunity
to wake up to the person
that we truly are at the core.
To live our lives
with heart and meaning,
to follow the yearning
of our soul, our dream
life purpose — to answer the call.

Little Buddha

Changing

It's amazing when you
haven't moved a muscle
or even taken a breath
and you find yourself
in a completely different

place.

Mount Sinai

Last Page

I thought recently, *God forbid I should
know what's going to happen in my life.*

There'd be no point in living it then.

Besides, you really piss off
the author when you skip to
the last page of the story.

The L:ittle Ones

Life's Crucible

I've come to realize that life's crucible is love.

Webster's defines crucible as
"1: a pot of very refractory
material used for melting and
calcining a substance that
requires a high degree of heat
2: a severe test."

I've also come to realize that within love
is the crucible of healing.

Webster's defines heal as
"1a: to make sound or whole."

Perhaps that's what the journey is all about.

Tripod

The Hard Part

Life's journey seems to begin
when you realize no matter what
you *think you're doing,*
the mystery of the process is *doing you.*

The hard part is waiting to find out
what you'll be like when *it's done.*

Lady Bug

Moments

Experience the moment where it is,
then leave it where it belongs.

Experience the moment
and let its echo resolve

so new moments can come.

Alter

Inner Altar

The deep inner alter of my soul
recognized its own reflection.

And my being held both
in equality and length.

The two worlds,
reaching for each
other for years
made material contact.

And I finally found
what I was looking for.

The rocks
and the flame
and the silence
had spoke the truth
after all.

Treblinka

Treblinka

There's nothing left but stones.

My Dad and I dedicated two
of them for his parents.

We stood there for some time
with the gentle breeze.

"I won't be back,"
he said, "but I'm glad I came."

I made a map of
where the two
stones were.

And I knew
some day
I would be
here again.

Father and Son

Full Circle

She asked him, "What is it like to sit
across from your son at this point in your life,
not having experienced that for yourself?"

My dad looked at me
and quietly said
with a soft smile,
"It feels good."

And tears welled up in my eyes as I realized
that I was able to be present for my dad in a
way he never received for himself, even as he sat in
the place his father never experienced having
been killed in the Warsaw Ghetto Uprising
when he was a boy.

And in some way the agonizing cross-generational
grief, loss, and pain had finally come full circle
and was healed in a sacred moment of connecting
with my father.
And as our stories merged, the story of his father
merged with him,
And then there was silence,
and I was finally with my dad.

We had both come home together.

About the Author

Born in Winnipeg, Manitoba, Joel Carter currently practices life and emergency medicine in Duluth, Minnesota. His soul continues to unfold in the good company of friends and family, under the watchful gaze of his four-leggeds and the Silent Ones.